Stand Out Basic

NESL 361

Jenkins | Johnson

Australia • Brazil • Japan • Korea • Mexico • Singapore • Spain • United Kingdom • United States

Stand Out Basic: NESL 361

Stand Out Basic, 3rd Edition
Jenkins | Johnson

© 2016 Cengage Learning. All rights reserved.

For product information and technology assistance, contact us at
Cengage Learning Customer & Sales Support, 1-800-354-9706

For permission to use material from this text or product,
submit all requests online at **cengage.com/permissions**
Further permissions questions can be emailed to
permissionrequest@cengage.com

This book contains select works from existing Cengage Learning resources and was produced by Cengage Learning Custom Solutions for collegiate use. As such, those adopting and/or contributing to this work are responsible for editorial content accuracy, continuity and completeness.

Compilation © 2017 Cengage Learning

ISBN: 978-1-337-69433-9

Cengage Learning
20 Channel Center Street
Boston, MA 02210
USA

Cengage Learning is a leading provider of customized learning solutions with office locations around the globe, including Singapore, the United Kingdom, Australia, Mexico, Brazil, and Japan. Locate your local office at: **www.international.cengage.com/region.**

Cengage Learning products are represented in Canada by Nelson Education, Ltd.

For your lifelong learning solutions, visit **www.cengage.com/custom.**

Visit our corporate website at **www.cengage.com.**

Brief Contents

Unit 1   Personal Information 12

Unit 2   Our Class 36

Unit 3   Food 60

Unit 4   Clothing 84

Personal Information

People line up to have their photo
taken for an art performance.

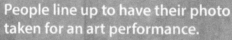

UNIT OUTCOMES

- [ ] Identify people
- [ ] Express nationalities
- [ ] Express marital status
- [ ] Say and write addresses
- [ ] Say and write dates

Look at the photo and answer the questions.

1. Where are the people in the pictures from?
2. How old are they?

GOAL ▢ Identify people

🎧 **A.** **IDENTIFY** **Listen and point.**

CD 1
TR 15

What's his name?
His name is Amal.

What's her name?
Her name is Ms. Adams.

What are their names?
Their names are Hang and Elsa.

What's your name?
My name is ...

B. **Practice the conversation. Use the questions in Exercise A to make new conversations.**

Student A: What's his name?
Student B: His name is Amal.

INTONATION
What's your name?
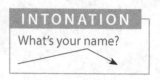

C. Listen and repeat.

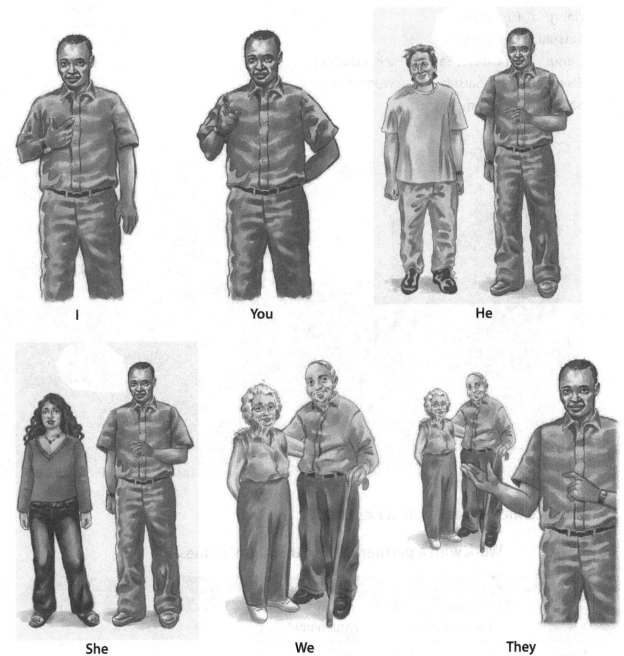

I

You

He

She

We

They

D. RELATE Look again at the pictures in Exercise A. Write.

1. His name is Amal. _____ He _____ is a student.

2. Her name is Ms. Adams. _____ is a teacher.

3. Their names are Hang and Elsa. _____ are students.

4. My name is _____, _____ am a student.

CD 1
TR 17

E. **Listen and point.**

Hang:	Hi, Satsuki.
Satsuki:	Hello, Hang.
Hang:	Elsa, this is Satsuki. He is a student.
Elsa:	Hello, Satsuki. I am a student, too.
Satsuki:	Nice to meet you.

F. **Practice the conversation in Exercise E.**

G. **CLASSIFY** **Work with a partner. Write classmates' names.**

Pronoun		Name
I	I am a student.	(your name)
You	You are a student.	(your partner's name)
He	He is a student.	
She	She is a student.	
We	We are students.	
They	They are students.	

LESSON **2** **Where are you from?**

GOAL ■ Express nationalities

🎧 **A. Read and listen.**
CD 1
TR 18

B. Write.

1. What's her name? _____

2. Where is she from? _____

C. Ask your classmates.

1. What's your name?

2. Where are you from?

D. SURVEY Ask about other classmates.

1. What's his name? What's her name?

2. Where's he from? Where's she from?

E. PREDICT Look at the picture and answer the questions.

1. Where is Shiro from? _____

2. Where is Amal from? _____

3. Where is Hang from? _____

4. Where is Elsa from? _____

CD 1
TR 19-23

F. Listen and write.

1. She is from Cuba. _____*Sara*_____

2. He is from Lebanon. _____

3. She is from Vietnam. _____

4. She is from Russia. _____

5. He is from Japan. _____

G. Practice the conversations. Use the information in Exercise F to make new conversations.

Student A: Where is <u>Sara</u> from?
Student B: She is from <u>Cuba</u>.

Student A: What's her birthplace?
Student B: <u>Cuba</u>.

> **BIRTHPLACE**
> Where is he from? He is from Japan.
> What's his birthplace? Japan.

H. Read.

Simple Present		
I	live	in Los Angeles.
He	lives	in Irvine.
She		in Chicago.

I. Complete the sentences.

1. Sara _is from Cuba_____. She _lives_____ in Irvine.

2. Shiro _____. He _____ in Irvine.

3. Amal _____. He _____ in Irvine.

4. Elsa _____. She _____ in Irvine.

5. Hang _____. She _____ in Irvine.

6. I am from _____. I _____.

J. Practice the conversation. Use the information in Exercise I to make new conversations.

CD 1
TR 24

Ms. Adams:	Hi, <u>Sara</u>. Where are you from?
Sara:	I'm from <u>Cuba</u>.
Ms. Adams:	Where do you live?
Sara:	I live in <u>Irvine</u>.

K. APPLY Ask four classmates. Make new conversations and complete the table.

You:	Hi, _____. Where are you from?
Classmate:	I'm from _____.
You:	Where do you live?
Classmate:	I live in _____.

Name (What's your name?)	Birthplace (Where are you from?)	Current city (Where do you live?)
1.		
2.		
3.		
4.		

LESSON 3 Are you married?

GOAL ▦ Express marital status

A. IDENTIFY Listen and write.

CD 1
TR 25

single	married	divorced

He is _____.

They are _____. They are _____.

B. With a partner, point at the pictures in Exercise A and say: *He is single, They are married,* or *They are divorced.*

C. Read.

The Verb *Be*			
Pronoun	**Be**	**Marital status**	**Example sentence**
I	am	married	I am married.
He	is	single	He is single. (Amed is single.)
She		divorced	She is divorced. (Mirna is divorced.)
We	are	divorced	We are divorced.
You		married	You are married.
They		single	They are single.

D. PREDICT Are they married, single, or divorced? Circle *yes* or *no*. Then, listen and write.

CD 1
TR 26

1.

Maria

Is she married?   Yes   No

She _____.

2.

Hans

Is he married?   Yes   No

He _____.

3.

Mr. and Mrs. Johnson

Are they married?   Yes   No

They _____.

E. Write *am*, *is*, or *are*.

1. Mr. and Mrs. Johnson _____*are*_____ married.

2. Orlando _____ divorced.

3. Omar, Natalie, and Doug _____ single.

4. We _____ divorced.

5. They _____ single.

6. She _____ married.

7. We _____ single.

8. You _____ married.

F. Read and write the contractions.

1. I + am = I'm	_____I'm_____ married.
2. You + are = You're	_____ divorced.
3. He + is = He's	_____ single.
4. She + is = She's	_____ divorced.
5. We + are = We're	_____ married.
6. They + are = They're	_____ single.

G. Complete the sentences with the verbs. Rewrite each sentence with a contraction.

1. We ____are____ married.   We're married. _____

2. They _____ divorced.   _____

3. I _____ single.   _____

4. He _____ divorced.   _____

5. You _____ married.   _____

6. She _____ single.   _____

H. Read.

A: Hans, are you married?   **A:** Lin, are you married?   **A:** Pam, are you married?
B: No, I'm single.   **B:** Yes, I'm married.   **B:** No, I'm divorced.

I. CLASSIFY Speak to five classmates.

Name	Marital status (Are you married?)
Hans	single
1.	
2.	
3.	
4.	
5.	

LESSON 4 What's your address?

A. Read.

IRVINE PUBLIC LIBRARY

FIRST NAME:	**Safa**
LAST NAME:	**Ahadi**
STREET ADDRESS:	**2687 Westpark Lane**
CITY:	**Irvine**
STATE:	**CA**
ZIP:	**92714**

B. Write.

First name: _Safa_

Last name: _Ahadi_

Street address: _____

City: _____

State: _____

Zip code: _____

C. IDENTIFY Listen and point to the addresses.

CD 1
TR 27

3259 Lincoln Street   51 Apple Avenue   12367 Elm Road

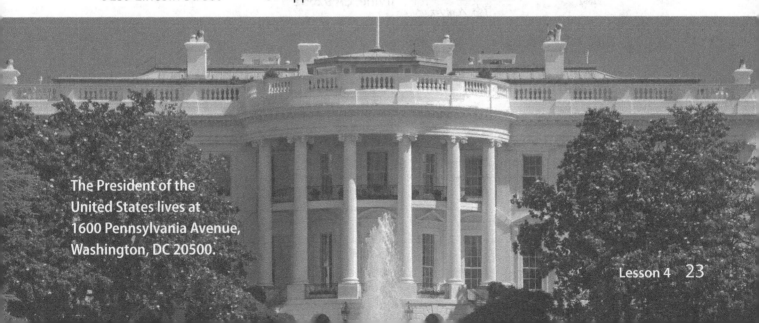

The President of the
United States lives at
1600 Pennsylvania Avenue,
Washington, DC 20500.

D. Listen to the addresses. Write the numbers only.

1. _____   2. _____   3. _____   4. _____

E. Listen and write.

> **COMMAS**
> Use commas (,) to separate the different parts of an address.

LOCKE ADULT SCHOOL

FIRST NAME:	**Amal**
LAST NAME:	**Jahshan**
STREET ADDRESS:	**8237 Augustin Street**
CITY:	**Irvine**
STATE:	**CA**
ZIP:	**92602**

Address:

_____*8237*_____ Augustin Street,

Irvine, CA 92602

IRVINE PUBLIC LIBRARY

FIRST NAME:	**Hang**
LAST NAME:	**Tran**
STREET ADDRESS:	_____ **Fin Road**
CITY:	**Irvine**
STATE:	**CA**
ZIP:	**92602**

x *Hang Tran*

Address:

_____ Fin Road,

Irvine, CA 92602

CUSTOMER SERVICES

FIRST NAME:	**Elsa**
LAST NAME:	**Kusmin**
STREET ADDRESS:	_____ **San Andrew Street**
CITY:	**Irvine**
STATE:	**CA**
ZIP:	**92602**

Elsa Kusmin

Address:

_____ San Andrew Street,

Irvine, CA 92602

F. **RELATE** Write the addresses.

Name	Address
Amal	*8237 Augustin Street, Irvine, CA 92602*
Hang	
Elsa	

G. Listen and read.

CD 1
TR 30

Hang: Hi, Amal. What's your address?

Amal: Hello, Hang. My address is 8237 Augustin Street, Irvine, California 92602.

Hang: Thanks.

The Verb *Be*		
Subject	**Be**	**Example Sentence**
He	is	He is a student.
She		She is a student.
It (address)		My address is 8237 Augustin Street, Irvine, California 92602.

H.   **Practice the conversations. Student A look at this page. Student B look at your answers in Exercise F. Write.**

Student A: Hi, Amal. What's your address?

Student B: Hello, Elsa. My address is 8237 Augustin Street, _____.

Student A: Thanks.

Student A: Hi, Elsa. What's your address?

Student B: Hello, Amal. My address is _____.

Student A: Thanks.

Student A: Hi, Hang. What's your address?

Student B: Hello, Amal. My address is _____.

Student A: Thanks.

I.   **APPLY** Ask your partner and write the information. Then ask two more classmates.

Name	Address

LESSON ⑤ What's your date of birth?

GOAL ▪ Say and write dates

A. Write this year. _____

B. LABEL Write the month and the year. Circle today's date.

		1	2	3	4	5
6	7	8	9	10	11	12
13	14	15	16	17	18	19
20	21	22	23	24	25	26
27	28	29	30	31		

C. Number the months.

January	February	March	April
01	_____	_____	_____

May	June	July	August
_____	_____	_____	_____

September	October	November	December
09	_____	_____	_____

🎧 **D.** **Listen to the months and say the number. Listen again and write the months**
CD 1
TR 31 **on a sheet of paper.**

December 5th, 1990: Norman Vaughn's 89th birthday, celebrated on Mount Vaughn.

E. Read.

Month	Day	Year	
September	21	2016	September 21st, 2016 09/21/2016
December	5	1990	December 5th, 1990 12/05/1990
August	2	1974	August 2nd, 1974 08/2/1974

ORDINAL NUMBERS

Notice how to write and say dates with words and numbers.

1st, 2nd, 3rd, 4th, 5th, 6th, 7th, 8th, 9th, 10th

January 1st	January 20th
January 2nd	January 21st
January 3rd	January 22nd
January 4th	January 30th
January 5th	January 31st

F. IDENTIFY Write the dates with words and numbers (December 5th, 1990).

1. The date today: _____

2. Your date of birth: _____

3. The date tomorrow: _____

4. Your friend's date of birth: _____

G. IDENTIFY Write the dates with numbers only (12/05/1990).

1. The date today: _____

2. Your date of birth: _____

3. The date tomorrow: _____

4. Your friend's date of birth: _____

H. **Listen and write the dates.**

Today	Date of birth
1.	
2.	
3.	

I. **APPLY** Practice the conversation. Use the information in Exercise H to make new conversations.

Student A: What's the date today?
Student B: It's <u>June 25th</u>.
Student A: Thanks.
Student A: What's your date of birth?
Student B: It's <u>July 3rd, 1988</u>.
Student A: Thanks.

CONTRACTIONS
What is = *What's*
It is = *It's*

J. **Develop a list of important class dates. Ask your teacher for help.**

1. Today's date: _____

2. First day of school: _____

3. Holidays: _____

_____

4. Last day of school: _____

July 4: Independence Day in the United States.

LIFESKILLS ▶ Nice to meet you

Before You Watch

A. **Look at the picture and answer the questions.**

1. Where are the people?
2. Who is the person standing at the front?

While You Watch

B. ▶ **Watch the video and circle the names you hear.**

Roger

Frank

Mateo

Edgar

Mrs. Smith

James

Hector

Linda

Naomi

Check Your Understanding

C. **Read the statements. Write *T* for true and *F* for false.**

1. Mrs. Smith is from California.   F

2. Hector lives in Boston.   _____

3. Mateo is from Puerto Rico.   _____

4. Naomi is from Pasadena.   _____

5. Naomi works in a diner.   _____

Review

A. Read.

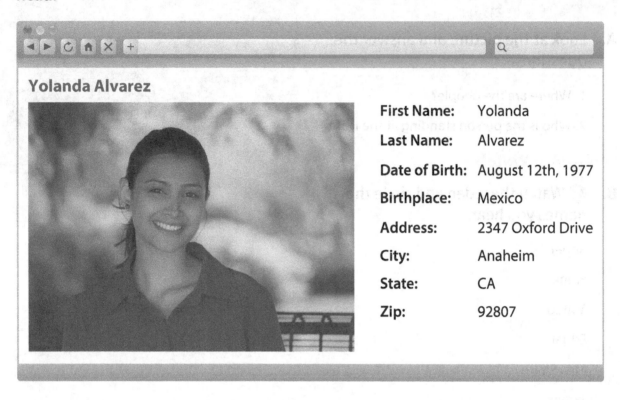

Yolanda Alvarez

First Name:	Yolanda
Last Name:	Alvarez
Date of Birth:	August 12th, 1977
Birthplace:	Mexico
Address:	2347 Oxford Drive
City:	Anaheim
State:	CA
Zip:	92807

B. Write.

1. What's her first name?

   _____

2. What's her last name?

   _____

3. What's her address?

   _____

4. What's her date of birth?

   _____

5. What's her birthplace?

   _____

C. Speak to a partner. Write.

What's your first name?   What's your last name?
What's your address?   What's your phone number?

Adult School Application

| Student Information>> | Household Information | Essay | Payment | Contact Us |

First Name

Last Name

Date of Birth   -Date-   -Month-   -Year-

Birthplace

Street Address

E-mail

City   -Select-

State   -Select-

Zip Code

Phone Number

Submit

D. Write.

| single | married | divorced |

_____   _____   _____

Learner Log

I can identify people.   I can express nationalities.
☐ Yes ☐ No ☐ Maybe   ☐ Yes ☐ No ☐ Maybe

E. Circle.

1.

She / He / They is from Germany.

2.

She / He / They is Ron Carter.

3.

She / He / They are in school.

4.

She / He / We live in Irvine.

F. Write the correct form of the verb *Be*. Then, write each sentence with a contraction.

1. She _____is_____ a student. _____ *She's a student.* _____

2. She _____ from Japan. _____

3. We _____ students at The Adult School. _____

4. They _____ from Honduras. _____

5. I _____ in school. _____

G. Write *live* or *lives*.

1. He _____ in Portugal.

2. I _____ in Chicago.

3. She _____ in the United States.

✓ **Make a class book**

Form a team with four or five students. In your team, you need:

Position	Job description	Student name
Student 1: Team Leader	Check that everyone speaks English. Check that everyone participates.	
Student 2: Writer	Write information.	
Student 3: Artist	Draw pictures.	
Students 4/5: Spokespeople	Organize presentation.	

1. Make a table like the one below.

2. Write the information for the members of your team.

What's your first name?	
What's your last name?	
What's your address?	
What's your phone number?	
What's your date of birth?	
What's your marital status?	

3. Draw a picture or add a photo of each member.

4. Make a team book.

5. Do a presentation about your team.

6. Make a class book with the other teams.

Jimmy Chin
Read more about Jimmy in Unit 5.

Sarah Marquis
Read more about Sarah in Unit 4.

Diana Nyad
Read more about Diana in Unit 6.

Maritza Morales Casanova
Read more about Maritza in Unit 8.

A. PREDICT Look at the pictures. Answer the questions.

1. Who lives in Mexico? _____

2. Who was born in 1973? _____

3. Who lives in Switzerland? _____

4. Who is from New York City? _____

B. **PREDICT** **Look at the pictures again. Put a check (✓) in the table.**

	Adventurer	Teacher	Swimmer	Climber
Sarah Marquis				
Jimmy Chin				
Diana Nyad				
Maritza Morales Casanova				

C. **Read about the explorers.**

Sarah Marquis

Sarah Marquis is from Switzerland. She is an adventurer and a National Geographic explorer. Her date of birth is June 20th, 1972.

Jimmy Chin

Jimmy Chin is from Mankato, Minnesota. He is a climber and photographer. He is also a National Geographic explorer. He was born in 1973.

Diana Nyad

Diana Nyad is from New York City. Her birth date is August 22nd, 1949. She is a swimmer and a National Geographic explorer.

Maritza Morales Casanova

Maritza Morales Casanova is a teacher and a National Geographic explorer. She is from Mexico. She was born in 1985.

D. **IDENTIFY** **Underline the date of birth in each paragraph.**

E. **CREATE** **Complete the sentences about the explorers.**

1. Sarah Marquis is an _____.

2. Jimmy Chin is from _____.

3. Diana Nyad is from _____.

4. Maritza Morales Casanova is a _____.

Our Class

University students
practice on models in
a dentistry class.

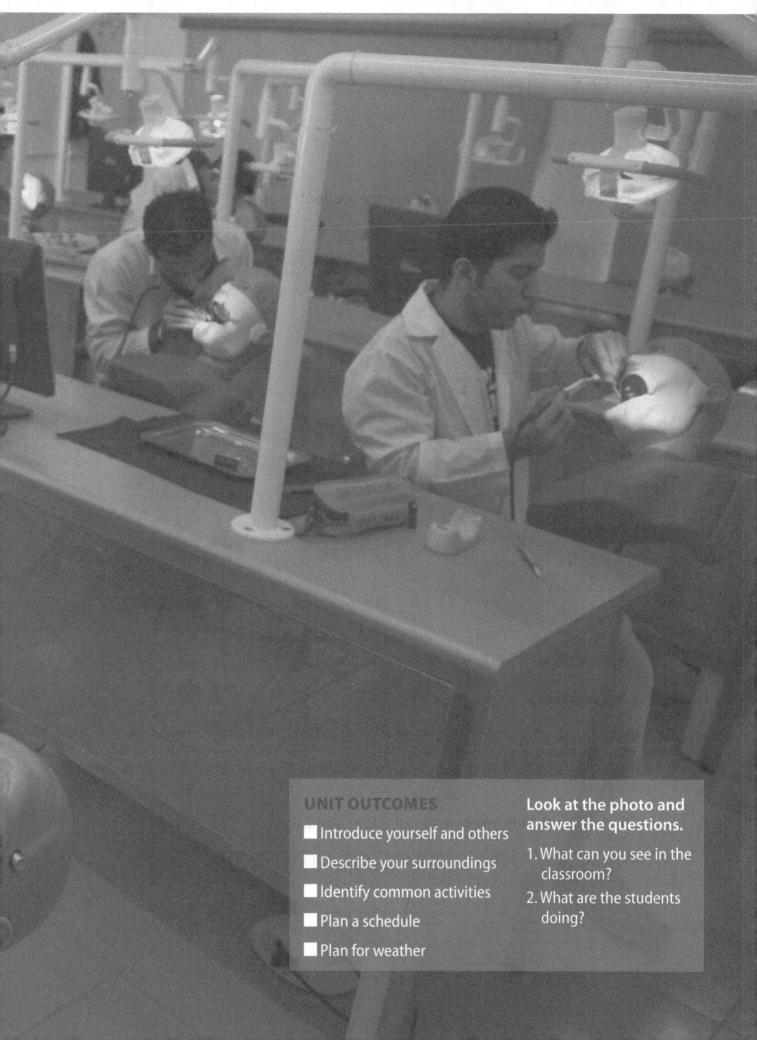

UNIT OUTCOMES

■ Introduce yourself and others

■ Describe your surroundings

■ Identify common activities

■ Plan a schedule

■ Plan for weather

Look at the photo and answer the questions.

1. What can you see in the classroom?

2. What are the students doing?

LESSON **1** Meet my friend

GOAL ▨ Introduce yourself and others

A. PREDICT Look at the picture. Where are the students from?

B. Listen and practice.

I want to introduce two new students today. This is Edgar. He is from Senegal. He lives in Sacramento. His phone number is (916) 555-3765.

Meet Julie. She is also a new student. She is from Canada. She lives in Folsom. Her number is (916) 555-4565.

C. CLASSIFY Write the information about Edgar and Julie.

Name	Phone	City
Edgar		
Julie		

D.   Read the chart.

Possessive Adjectives		
Subject	**Possessive adjective**	**Example sentence**
I	My	**My** phone number is 555-3456.
You	Your	**Your** address is 2359 Maple Drive.
He	His	**His** name is Edgar.
She	Her	**Her** name is Julie.
We	Our	**Our** last name is Perez.
They	Their	**Their** teacher is Mr. Jackson.

E.   RELATE Look at the pictures and complete the sentences.

This is Mr. Jackson. _____ phone number is 555-2813.

_____ address is 3317 Maple Drive.

Irma and Edgar are married. _____ phone

number is 555-3765. _____ address is 1700

Burns Avenue.

F.   Complete the sentences.

1. John is single. _____ address is 3215 Park Street.

2. You're a student here. _____ phone number is 555-2121, right?

3. We're from Russia. _____ address is 1652 Main Street.

4. I'm a new student. _____ name is Julie.

G. Learn the introductions.

This is …	This is Oscar.
Meet …	Meet Julie.
I want to introduce …	I want to introduce Edgar.

H. Listen and circle.

1. This is …	Meet …	I want to introduce …
2. This is …	Meet …	I want to introduce …
3. This is …	Meet …	I want to introduce …

INTONATION

What's your name?

What's your phone number?

What's your address?

I. SURVEY Talk to four classmates.

Name (What's your name?)	Phone number (What's your phone number?)	Address (What's your address?)
1.		
2.		
3.		
4.		

J. Introduce a classmate to the class.

LESSON ② Where's the pencil sharpener?

GOAL ▪ Describe your surroundings

CD 1
TR 35

A. Listen and repeat. Point to the picture.

trash can	file cabinets	board	bookcase	plant	door

B. LOCATE Write: *desk, computer, chair,* and *book.*

CD 1
TR 36

C. Listen and point.

D. RELATE Ask questions. Use the words in Exercise A.

EXAMPLE: **Where's the trash can?**

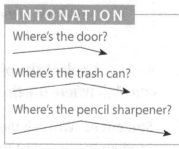

INTONATION

Where's the door?

Where's the trash can?

Where's the pencil sharpener?

E. Read.

Prepositions of Location

Where's the desk?

It's **behind** the chair.

Where's the plant?

It's **on** the desk.

Where's the trash can?

It's **between** the desk and the bookcase.

Where are the file cabinets?

They're **next to** the computer.

Where are the students?

They're **in front of** the board.

Where are the books?

They're **in** the bookcase.

F. APPLY Look at the picture in Exercise B. Ask *where is the teacher, plant,* and *trash can.* Ask *where are the file cabinets, students,* and *books.*

Student A: Where is the teacher?
Student B: He is next to the door.

Student A: Where are the file cabinets?
Student B: They are behind the computers.

G. CREATE Draw your classroom.

H. Write.

1. Where is the teacher's desk? _____

2. Where is the trash can? _____

3. Where is the board? _____

4. Where are the books? _____

5. Where are the file cabinets? _____

GOAL   ▨ Identify common activities

🎧 **A.** **Listen and point to the students.**

CD 1
TR 37

Shiro

Sara

Julie

Edgar

B. **IDENTIFY** **Write the names of the students.**

1. listen   _____

2. read   _____

3. write   _____

4. talk   _____

C. Read the words and find examples in your classroom.

| pen | clock | board | ~~pencil~~ | book | notebook | CD | magazine | teacher |

D. IDENTIFY Write the words from Exercise C.

1.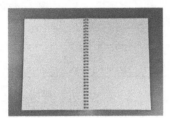

pencil

2.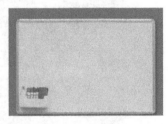

3.

4.

5.

6.

7.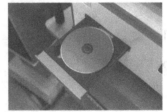

8.

9.

E. CLASSIFY Complete the table with the objects in Exercise D.

Write	Listen	Read

F. Read.

Present Continuous				
He She	is	read write listen talk sit stand	-ing	He is reading. / She is reading. He is writing. / She is writing. He is listening. / She is listening. He is talking. / She is talking. He is sitting. / She is sitting. He is standing. / She is standing.

G. Write.

1. She is reading. _____
2. She is listening. _____

3. He _____
4. He _____

5. _____
6. _____

H. REPORT Write about your classmates.

1. Juan is sitting. _____
2. _____
3. _____
4. _____
5. _____

LESSON ④ When's English class?

GOAL ▓ Plan a schedule

CD 1
TR 38

🎧 **A. Read and listen.**

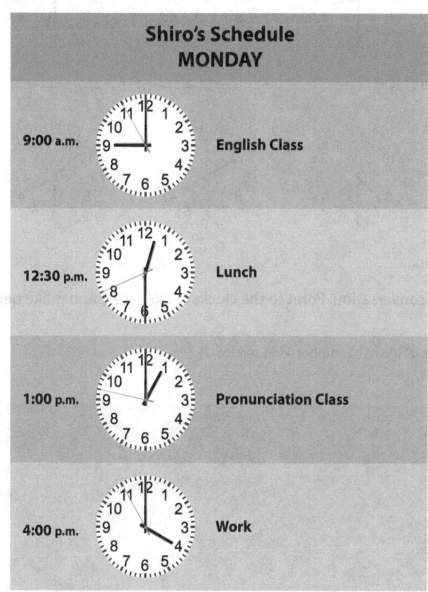

Shiro's Schedule
MONDAY

9:00 a.m.   English Class

12:30 p.m.   Lunch

1:00 p.m.   Pronunciation Class

4:00 p.m.   Work

INTONATION

When's English class?

When's lunch?

When's pronunciation class?

B. IDENTIFY Look at Shiro's schedule.

1. When's English class? ___It's at nine o'clock._____

2. When's lunch? _____

3. When's pronunciation class? _____

4. When's work? _____

C. What time is it? Write.

1.
It's ___3:00___.

2.
It's ___3:30___.

3.
It's _____.

4.
It's _____.

5.
It's _____.

6.
It's _____.

7.
It's _____.

8.
It's _____.

D. RELATE Practice the conversation. Point to the clocks in Exercise C and make new conversations.

Student A: What time is it? (Point to number 4 in Exercise C.)
Student B: It's <u>five thirty</u>.

It's one thirty at Grand Central Station in New York City.

E. Listen and write.

CD 1
TR 39

Julie's Schedule
MONDAY

9:00 a.m.	English Class
_____	Work
_____	Lunch
_____	Dinner
_____	Bedtime

F. Listen and read.

CD 1
TR 40

Julie: When's English class?
Mr. Jackson: It's at nine o'clock.
Julie: What time is it now?
Mr. Jackson: It's seven thirty.

G. Practice the conversation in Exercise F. Make new conversations.

A: When's _____?

B: It's _____.

A: What time is it now?

B: It's _____.

H. PLAN Write your schedule on a separate piece of paper.

LESSON 5 It's cold today

GOAL   Plan for weather

A. Listen and repeat.

CD 1
TR 41

| windy | cloudy | foggy | rainy | snowy | cold | hot | sunny |

B. IDENTIFY Listen and write the words from Exercise A.

CD 1
TR 42

Montreal, Canada
_____

Havana, Cuba
hot
_____

San Francisco, United States
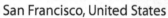

Patagonia, Chile
_____

Tokyo, Japan
_____

New York City, United States
_____

C. Review the weather.

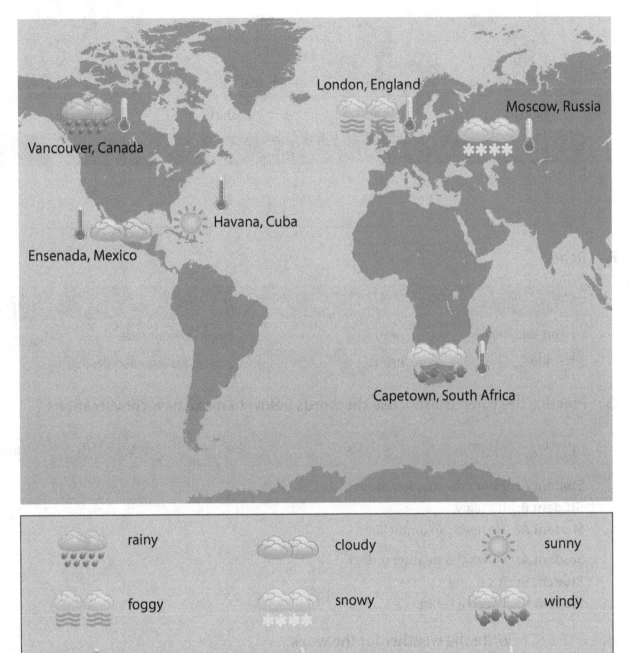

	rainy		cloudy		sunny
	foggy		snowy		windy
	hot		warm		cold

D. **RELATE** Practice the conversation. Use the information in Exercise C to make new conversations.

A: How's the weather in <u>Havana, Cuba</u> today?

B: It's <u>hot and sunny</u>.

E. **CLASSIFY** Write the correct clothes for the weather.

sandals

boots

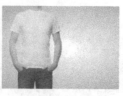
a t-shirt

an umbrella

Rainy	Sunny

F. **Read.**

Simple Present		
I, You, We, They	need	I **need** an umbrella.
He, She	needs	She **needs** an umbrella.

G. **Practice the conversation. Use the words below to make new conversations.**

I	You	He	She	We	They

Student A: How's the weather today?
Student B: It's rainy.
Student A: He needs an umbrella.

Student A: How's the weather today?
Student B: It's sunny.
Student A: I need a t-shirt.

H. **PREDICT** Write the weather for the week.

Monday	Tuesday	Wednesday	Thursday	Friday	Saturday	Sunday

I. **Look on the Internet or in a newspaper. Check the weather for the week and compare it with your predictions in Exercise H.**

Before You Watch

A. **Look at the picture and answer the questions.**

1. Where are Hector, Mateo, and Naomi?

2. What's the weather like? How do you know?

While You Watch

B. ▶ **Watch the video and circle the words you hear.**

boots

umbrella

poncho

snowy

rainy

windy

cold

bad weather

cloudy

Check Your Understanding

C. **Put the events in order.**

1. _____ Mateo enters.

2. _____ Naomi, Hector, and Mateo run outside.

3. __1__ Hector enters.

4. _____ Naomi enters.

5. _____ Naomi, Hector, and Mateo talk about the weather.

Review

A. Read.

B. Complete.

I want to introduce _____ and _____. They are from _____.

_____ address is _____.

_____ phone number is _____.

C. Ask a classmate for information. Introduce your classmate to another student.

Learner Log

I can plan for weather.   I can plan a schedule.
☐ Yes ☐ No ☐ Maybe   ☐ Yes ☐ No ☐ Maybe

D. Read.

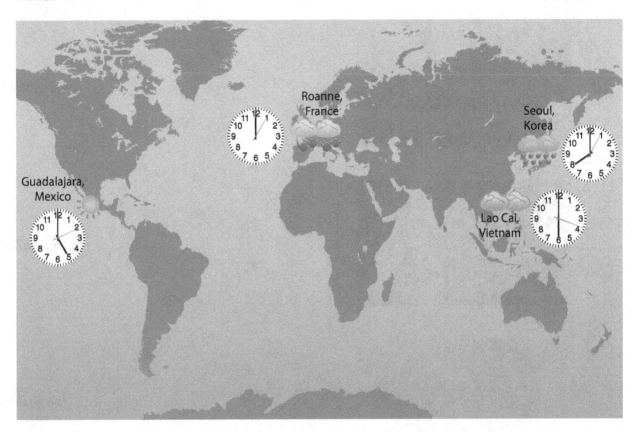

E. Write.

1. How's the weather in Korea? _It's rainy in Korea._

   What time is it? _It's 8:00._

2. How's the weather in France? _____

   What time is it? _____

3. How's the weather in Mexico? _____

   What time is it? _____

4. How's the weather in Vietnam? _____

   What time is it? _____

Learner Log

I can identify common activities.   I can describe my surroundings.
☐ Yes   ☐ No   ☐ Maybe   ☐ Yes   ☐ No   ☐ Maybe

F. Match.

1.

        a. He is listening.

2.

        b. He is writing.

3.

        c. She is talking.

4.

        d. He is reading.

G. Write.

 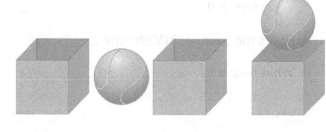

    in   _____   _____   _____

TEAM PROJECT ✓ Make a display

COLLABORATE Form a team with four or five students. In your team, you need:

Position	Job description	Student name
Student 1: Team Leader	Check that everyone speaks English. Check that everyone participates.	
Student 2: Writer	Help team members write.	
Student 3: Artist	Arrange a display with help from the team.	
Students 4/5: Spokespeople	Prepare a presentation.	

1. Draw a picture of yourself.
   Draw a map of your country.
   Draw a clock with the time in your country.
   Draw the weather in your country.

2. Present each student's work in your group to the class.

What time is it in your country?

EXPLORER JOE RIIS

A Busy Schedule

"I wake up really early in my tent ... then start my 18-hour workday of photographing wildlife and science."
—Joe Riis

A. PREDICT Look at the picture. Answer the questions.

1. Where is Joe? What is he doing?

2. Look at what Joe is wearing. What's the weather like?

B. **PREDICT** What time does Joe do the following activities? Put a check (✓) in the table for each question.

	10:00 p.m.	6:00 a.m.	8:00 a.m.
What time does he wake up?			
What time does he take photos?			
What time does he go to bed?			

C. Read the interview with Joe Riis.

Joe Riis is a widlife photojournalist. He takes photos of wild animals and tells stories using his pictures.

Interviewer: Joe, you have a busy schedule, so thank you for your time. Can you tell us what you do?

Joe: Sure. I take photos of wild animals. I share the photos with people so they can connect with the planet.

Interviewer: What time do you wake up?

Joe: I wake up in my tent at 6:00 a.m.

Interviewer: What time do you take photos?

Joe: I take photos all day! I start at 8:00 a.m.

Interviewer: What do you do next?

Joe: I talk with people to get information I need to tell stories with my photos.

Interviewer: What time do you go to bed?

Joe: I go to bed at 10:00 p.m.

D. **IDENTIFY** Circle the times. Look again at Exercise B. Is your table correct?

E. **RELATE** Complete the sentences about yourself.

1. My class is at _____.

2. I eat lunch at _____.

3. My English class is at _____.

4. I _____ at _____.

Food

SH FACTS TO MUNCH ON:

People at a party enjoy meals
from a food truck.

UNIT OUTCOMES

- [ ] Identify common foods
- [ ] Express hunger
- [ ] Plan meals
- [ ] Make a shopping list
- [ ] Express preferences

Look at the photo and answer the questions.

1. What food can you buy from this food truck?
2. What's your favorite food?

GOAL ◼ Identify common foods

A. Look at the picture. Where are the students?

🎧 **B. RELATE** Listen and read the conversation. Use the words below to make new
CD 1
TR 43 conversations.

a chicken sandwich	a tuna fish sandwich	a ham sandwich

Andre: The food looks good!
Silvina: Yes, it does.
Andre: What are you eating?
Silvina: A <u>turkey sandwich</u>.

C. **IDENTIFY** Listen and point.

CD 1
TR 44

apples	butter	eggs	milk	tomatoes
bananas	cheese	lettuce	oranges	turkey
bread	chicken	mayonnaise	potatoes	water

D. **Match the letters in the picture to the food words. Write the words.**

a. _____milk_____   b. _____   c. _____

d. _____   e. _____   f. _____

g. _____   h. _____   i. _____

j. _____   k. _____   l. _____

m. _____   n. _____   o. _____

E. **Look and read.**

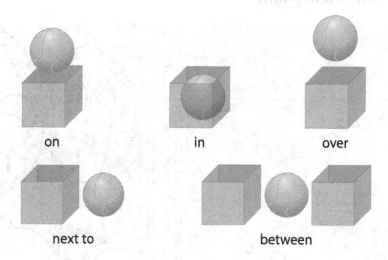

on in over

next to between

F. **CLASSIFY** **Look at the picture in Exercise C. Write the foods in the table.**

on the counter	*in* the refrigerator	*over* the counter
bread		

G. **Look at the picture in Exercise C again. Complete the sentences with *next to* or *between*.**

1. The water is _____ the milk.

2. The turkey is _____ the bread and the cheese.

3. The mayonnaise is _____ the chicken.

4. The cheese is _____ the turkey and the tomatoes.

H. **Practice the conversation. Use the picture in Exercise C to make new conversations.**

A: Where's the <u>bread</u>?
B: It's <u>next to the turkey</u>.

I. **APPLY** **Make a list of foods in your refrigerator on a sheet of paper and share it with a partner.**

LESSON ② I'm hungry!

GOAL ■ Express hunger

A. Look at the picture. Where are Saul and Chen?

🎧 **B. Listen and read.**
CD 1
TR 45

Saul: I'm hungry.
Chen: Me, too.
Saul: What's for dinner?
Chen: <u>Chicken and vegetables</u>.

C. RELATE Practice the conversation in Exercise B. Use the meals below to make new conversations.

chicken
sandwiches

hamburgers
and fries

tacos

rice and vegetables

D. **Read about Saul and Chen. Then, read the chart.**

Saul is hungry. He is not thirsty.

Chen is thirsty. He is not hungry.

The Verb *Be*			
Subject	***Be***		**Example sentence**
I	am (not)		I am (I'm) hungry. I am not (I'm not) hungry.
He	is (not)	hungry thirsty	He is (He's) thirsty. He is not (He's not) thirsty.
She			She is (She's) hungry. She is not (She's not) hungry.
We	are (not)		We are (We're) thirsty. We are not (We're not) thirsty.
You			You are (You're) hungry. You are not (You're not) hungry.
They			They are (They're) thirsty. They are not (They're not) thirsty.

E. **RELATE** **Write. Follow the example sentences in the chart.**

1. Edgar _____ is _____ hungry.

   He's not thirsty.
   _____

2. Roselia and Thanh _____ thirsty.

   _____

3. We _____ hungry.

   _____

4. She _____ not hungry.

   _____

5. I _____ thirsty.

   _____

6. You _____ not hungry.

   _____

F. **Read and listen.**

carrots

oranges

apples

chips

cookies

milk

water

G. **IDENTIFY** **Listen and write.**

1. _____carrots_____

2. _____

3. _____

4. _____

H. **Practice.**

Student A: What's your favorite snack?

Student B: My favorite snack is <u>cookies</u>.

I. **SURVEY** **Ask your classmates about their favorite snacks. Use the conversation in Exercise H.**

Name	Food

LESSON ③ Let's have spaghetti!

GOAL ▒ Plan meals

A. Look at the recipe. Read the ingredients.

Spaghetti and Meatballs

Ingredients: *Serves 6 people*
2 jars of tomato sauce
2 eggs
1 onion
1 package of spaghetti
2 pounds of ground beef
salt
pepper

Instructions:
1. Combine the beef, eggs, chopped onion, salt, and pepper in a large bowl.
2. Make mixture into balls and bake for 15 minutes.
3. Cook the pasta according to package directions.
4. Heat tomato sauce and add meatballs.
5. Serve spaghetti and sauce together.

B. Write.

1. How many jars of tomato sauce do you need? _____*two jars*_____

2. How many eggs do you need? _____

3. How many onions do you need? _____

4. How many packages of spaghetti do you need? _____

5. How many pounds of ground beef do you need? _____

C. IDENTIFY Listen and circle.

CD 1
TR 51-54

1. jar   package   pound

2. jar   package   pound

3. jar   package   pound

4. jar   package   pound

D. Read the chart. Listen and repeat.

CD 1
TR 55

Singular and Plural Nouns	
Singular	**Plural**
jar	jars
can	cans
bag	bags
package	packages
pound	pounds
Exceptions potato tomato sandwich	 potato**es** tomato**es** sandwich**es**

E. **CONSTRUCT** **Practice the conversation. Complete the table and make new conversations.**

Student A: What do we need?
Student B: We need <u>apples</u>.

PLURALS		
/s/	/z/	/iz/
chip**s**	jar**s**	packag**es**
carrot**s**	can**s**	orang**es**

Fruit		Vegetables	
apple	/z/ apples	carrot	/s/
orange	/iz/	tomato	/z/
banana	/z/	potato	/z/
pear	/z/	pepper	/z/

F. Write the food words and the quantities.

four cookies

G. **RELATE** Practice the conversation. Use the pictures to make new conversations.

Student A: What are the ingredients?
Student B: Two eggs and one onion.

1.   2.   3.   4.

H. **PLAN** Work in a group. Think of more fruits to make a fruit salad.

Fruit Salad		
Ingredients *Serves 6 people*	1 banana	___ _____
	2 apples	___ _____
	___ pear	___ _____
	___ orange	___ _____

LESSON 4 What's for dinner?

GOAL ■ Make a shopping list

CD 1
TR 56

A. Listen and point.

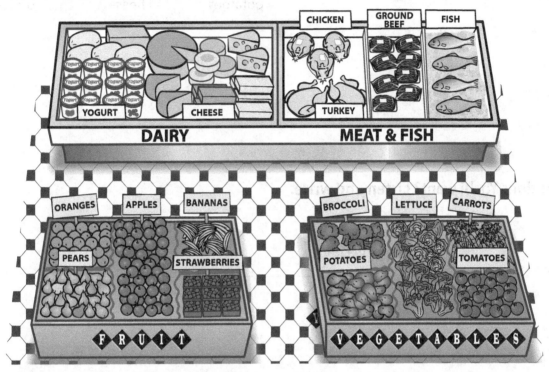

B. CLASSIFY Write the words in the correct shopping lists.

Meat and Fish	Vegetables	Fruit	Dairy
1. ground beef	1.	1.	1.
2.	2.	2.	2.
3.	3.	3.	
4.	4.	4.	
	5.	5.	

C. Complete the shopping lists with your own ideas.

D. **Read Amadeo's shopping list.**

Shopping List	
apples	tomatoes
water	chicken
milk	eggs
carrots	chips
cheese	

E. **LOCATE** **What does Amadeo want? Circle the items.**

oranges	apples	eggs
potatoes	cheese	broccoli

CD 1
TR 57

F. **What does Yoshi want? Listen and write.**

Shopping List		
oranges		

Farmers markets sell local food products.

G. Read.

Simple Present		
Subject	**Verb**	**Example sentence**
I, You, We, They	want	They **want** apples.
He, She	wants	She **wants** apples.
		He **wants** apples.

H. COMPARE Look at Amadeo's and Yoshi's shopping lists in exercises D and F. Complete the diagram.

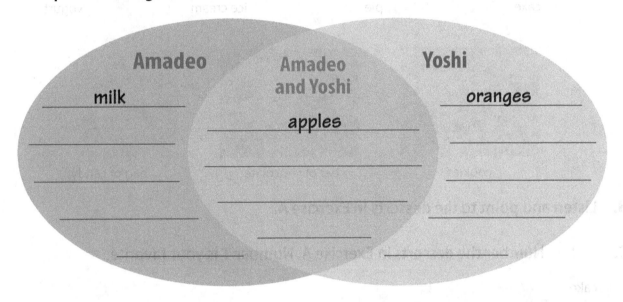

Amadeo

milk

_____

_____

_____

Amadeo and Yoshi

apples

_____

_____

_____

_____

Yoshi

oranges

_____

_____

I. What do you want? Make a list.

Shopping List

J. What does your partner want? Ask your partner and write.

Shopping List

K. Share your partner's information with a group.

LESSON **5** **What do you like?**

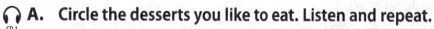

GOAL ▪ Express preferences

 A. **Circle the desserts you like to eat. Listen and repeat.**

CD 1
TR 58

cake	pie	ice cream	yogurt

cookies	bar of chocolate	bag of candy

 B. **Listen and point to the desserts in Exercise A.**

CD 1
TR 59–61

C. **RANK** **Number the desserts in Exercise A. Number 1 is your favorite.**

cake _____

pie _____

ice cream _____

yogurt _____

cookies _____

chocolate _____

candy _____

 D. **Listen and take notes. Write what Maria likes.**

CD 1
TR 62

1. Maria likes _____.

2. She likes _____.

3. She likes _____.

E. **Read the chart.**

Simple Present		
Subject	**Verb**	**Example sentence**
I, You, We, They	like	I **like** ice cream.
	eat	We **eat** ice cream.
	want	They **want** ice cream.
He, She	likes	She **likes** chocolate.
	eats	He **eats** chocolate.
	wants	She **wants** chocolate.

F. **Write the verb.**

1. I _____ (want) apple pie.

2. Maria _____*likes*_____ (like) ice cream.

3. You _____ (eat) pie.

4. They _____ (eat) cookies.

5. We _____ (like) fruit.

6. Saul _____ (like) candy.

7. We _____ (want) yogurt.

8. I _____ (like) _____.

G. **IDENTIFY** **Write about the pictures.**

1. _She wants cookies._____ 2. _____ 3. _____

H. Read.

Student A: Do you like <u>ice cream</u> for dessert?
Student B: No, I like <u>pie</u>.

I. **Practice the conversation in Exercise H. Use the words in Exercise A to make new conversations.**

J. **COMPARE** **What desserts does your partner like? Complete the diagram.**

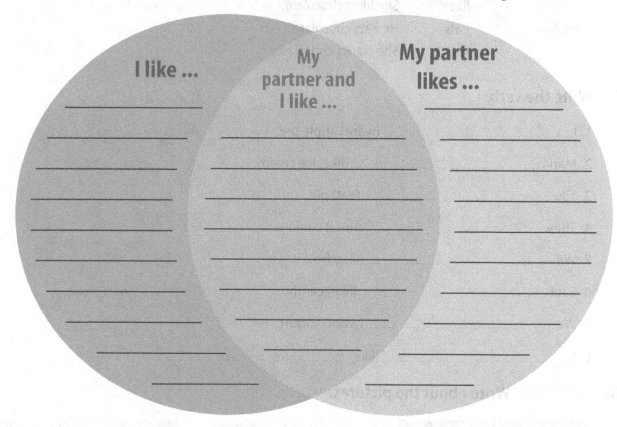

K. **Tell your classmates about your partner.**

LIFESKILLS ▶ What's for lunch?

Before You Watch

A. **Look at the picture and answer the questions.**

1. Where are Hector and Mateo?

2. What do you think they are going to eat?

While You Watch

B. ▶ **Watch the video and circle what Hector and Mateo order.**

Mateo	Hector
1. a. chicken soup b. chicken salad	4. a. taco b. cheeseburger
2. a. iced coffee b. iced tea	5. a. fried rice b. French fries
3. a. chocolate pie b. chocolate cake	6. a. onion rings b. chicken salad

Check Your Understanding

C. **Match the questions to the answers.**

Server	Customer
1. How are you?	a. Chocolate cake for me, please.
2. Do you need some more time to look at the menu?	b. No, I'm ready to order.
3. What would you like?	c. I'll have the special.
4. Do you want something to drink?	d. Great. I'm really hungry.
5. Would you like anything for dessert?	e. Yes, I'll have an iced tea with no sugar.

Review

A. Write the food words.

_____

_____

_____

_____

_____

_____

B. Write the plural food words.

Singular	Plural
apple	
orange	
chicken	
banana	
cookie	
egg	
chip	
potato	
tomato	
carrot	

C. Write *am, is,* or *are.*

1. Maria _____ thirsty.

2. Kim and David _____ not hungry.

3. Lan and Mai _____ hungry.

4. Rafael _____ not thirsty.

5. Colby _____ hungry.

6. Marco and Eva _____ thirsty.

7. Lara _____ not hungry.

8. I _____ thirsty.

D. Write negative sentences.

1. Eric is hungry.   He's not thirsty.

2. Maria is thirsty.   _____

3. Saul and Chen are hungry.   _____

4. I am thirsty.   _____

E. Write the simple present.

1. Chrissy _____ (like) hamburgers.

2. You _____ (eat) tacos.

3. Laura _____ (want) vegetables.

4. Rosie and Amadeo _____ (like) rice.

5. We _____ (eat) fish and chicken.

6. They _____ (want) pie.

7. Karl _____ (like) oranges.

8. I _____.

F. Talk to two classmates. Ask: *What do you want?*

Shopping List

Shopping List

G. Read the lists in Exercise F. Write.

Singular Foods	Plural Foods

1. **COLLABORATE** Form a team with four or five students. In your team, you need:

Position	Job description	Student name
Student 1: Team Leader	Check that everyone speaks English. Check that everyone participates.	
Student 2: Writer	Write food names.	
Student 3: Artist	Draw pictures for the shopping list with help from the team.	
Students 4/5: Spokespeople	Prepare a presentation.	

2. You are a family. What is your last name?

3. Make a shopping list with food from this unit.

4. Draw pictures of the food on your list.

5. Present your list to the class.

Shopping lists are different in other parts of the world.

A Recipe for Success

"...become involved in what you eat, grow, and plant, and make an effort to connect with other people ..."
—Catherine Jaffee

A. PREDICT Look at the picture. Answer the questions.

1. What are the people in the picture wearing?

2. What food do you think the article will be about? Why?

3. Do you think Catherine likes her job? Why?

Some kinds of honey bees are disappearing. Balyolu helps the Caucasian honey bee to survive.

B. FIND OUT Circle the correct answers.

1. A *Project* is a . . .
   a. plan of work
   b. vacation

2. A *leader* is a person who . . .
   a. guides others
   b. makes honey

3. *An expert* is a person who . . .
   a. knows a little
   b. knows a lot

4. *Beekeepers* are people who . . .
   a. work with people
   b. work with bees

C. Read about Catherine Jaffee.

Catherine Jaffee is a food *expert*. She has a very important job. She helps communities to be successful through food. Balyolu—one of Catherine's projects—helps *beekeepers* in Turkey to make honey and teaches them how to be business *leaders*. This *project* also helps to care for bees.

Some people put honey in yogurt; some people put it on their toast. However you use honey, Catherine is working to make sure it stays on your shopping list.

D. CLASSIFY Complete the chart about the story.

Person	Food	Insect	Place
Catherine Jaffee			

E. Read the shopping list.

Summer Salad with Honey

1 package of spinach

1 cup of strawberries

1 small onion

1/2 cup of blueberries

1/4 cup of cheese

honey

F. APPLY Find a meal that contains honey. Write a shopping list.

UNIT (4)

Clothing

Clothing comes in many different styles and colors.

UNIT OUTCOMES

- Identify types of clothing
- Ask for and give directions in a store
- Describe clothing
- Make purchases
- Read advertisements

Look at the photo and answer the questions.

1. What types of clothing can you see?
2. What colors are the clothes?

LESSON **1** What's on sale?

GOAL ■ Identify types of clothing

CD 1
TR 63

A. **IDENTIFY** Listen and point to the clothing.

CD 1
TR 64

B. **Listen to the conversation and read.**

Salesperson: May I help you?
Maria: Yes, I want a shirt, pants, a sweater, and shoes.

C. **Read the conversation in Exercise B again. Write sentences.**

1. _She wants a shirt._____.

2. _____.

3. _____.

4. _____.

D. IDENTIFY What clothes can you see in the ad?

E. Listen and write the number of the conversation.

CD 1
TR 65

A PAIR OF ...
Use *a pair of* with clothes that have two parts (socks, gloves). *A pair of* can also be used with clothes that have two legs (pants, shorts).

____ _____

____ _____

____ _____

1   _____blouse_____

____ _____

____ _____

____ _____

____ _____

F. Write the types of clothing for each picture in Exercise E.

~~blouse~~	socks	dress	shirt	pants	sweater	coat	shorts

G. Read.

Simple Present: *Have*		
Subject	*Have*	**Example sentence**
I, You, We, They	have	I **have** two shirts. I **have** a pair of socks.
He, She	has	She **has** a dress. She **has** a pair of shoes.

H. Write.

1. (blouse)　She _has a blouse_ _____.

　(shoes)　He _has shoes_____. **or** He _has a pair of shoes_____.

2. (dress)　She _____.

3. (coats)　They _____.

4. (socks)　I _____. **or** I _____.

5. (sweaters)　We _____.

6. (pants)　You _____. **or** You _____.

I. What's in Maria's closet? Write.

3 _____

1 pair of _____

1 _____

J. LIST What's in your closet? Write four items.

_____　　_____

_____　　_____

LESSON ② Where's the fitting room?

GOAL ▪ Ask for and give directions in a store

A. Listen and point.

CD 1
TR 66

B. CLASSIFY Look at the picture in Exercise A and write the clothes.

Men's	Women's	Children's	Teen Boys'	Teen Girls'
		hats		skirts

C. Read.

Prepositions of Location	
a. It's **in the front of** the store. b. It's **in the corner of** the store. c. It's **in the middle of** the store. d. It's **in the back of** the store. e. It's **on the left side of** the store. f. It's **on the right side of** the store.	

D. Look at the picture in Exercise A. Answer the questions.

1. Where's the fitting room? _It's in the back of the store._

2. Where's the men's section? _____

3. Where's the women's section? _____

4. Where's the children's section? _____

5. Where's the teen boys' section? _____

6. Where's the teen girls' section? _____

E. RELATE Listen and practice the conversation. Make new conversations. (Student A looks at Exercise D and Student B looks at the picture in Exercise A.)

CD 1
TR 67

Student A: Can you help me?
Student B: Sure. What can I do for you?
Student A: Where's the <u>fitting room?</u>
Student B: It's <u>in the back of the store.</u>
Student A: Thank you.

F. Listen and point.

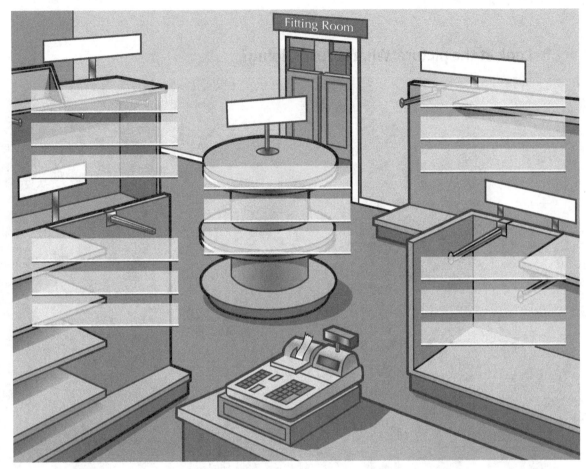

Fitting Room

G. Listen and write the sections in the picture.

H. CREATE In a group, write clothing in the picture for each section.

new arrival

The men's section of a clothing store

LESSON ③ What colors do you like?

GOAL ▨ Describe clothing

A. INFER Look at the picture. What is Yusuf doing?

B. Listen and read.

CD 1
TR 70

Salesperson:	Can I help you?
Yusuf:	Yes, I want a shirt.
Salesperson:	What color do you like—white, blue, or red?
Yusuf:	I don't know, maybe blue.

YES/NO QUESTIONS

Can I help you?

May I help you?

Do you need help?

C. Listen and repeat. Read the colors in the picture.

CD 1
TR 71

white
green
gray
orange
red

black
purple
pink
blue
yellow
brown

ADJECTIVE POSITION
A blue tie (correct)

A tie blue (not correct)

D. Listen and point to the clothing items.

CD 1
TR 72

| S = Small | M = Medium | L = Large | XL = Extra Large |

E. CLASSIFY Look at Exercise D. Complete the inventory.

Adel's Inventory List			
Quantity (How many?)	Item	Size	Color
	shirt	S	
2	shirt	M	
1	shirt	L	
2	shirt		

Lesson 3   93

F. Read.

Singular	Plural
There **is** one green shirt. There**'s** one green shirt.	There **are** two black shirts.

G. Practice the conversation. Use the information in Exercise E to make new conversations.

Student A: How many <u>white</u> shirts are there?
Student B: There's <u>one</u>.

H. CREATE Write an inventory for your class. Write about your classmates' clothing.

Class Inventory		
Quantity (How many?)	Item	Color

I. CREATE Write an inventory of the clothes in your closet.

LESSON 4 That's $5.00

GOAL ▪ Make purchases

🎧 CD 1 TR 73

A. IDENTIFY Listen and point to the cash registers.

1.

2.

3.

B. Circle the correct number from Exercise A.

1. one dollar	1	2	3
2. ten dollars and forty-one cents	1	2	3
3. six dollars and twenty-five cents	1	2	3

🎧 CD 1 TR 74

C. Listen and read with your teacher.

a dollar bill	a dollar coin $1.00	a quarter $.25	a dime $.10	a nickel $.05	a penny $.01

D. **RELATE** Match the amounts with the money.

1. $.50

a.

2. $15.08

b.

3. $35.10

c.

E. **Practice the conversations with a partner.**

Student A: How much is the shirt?
Student B: It's $15.00.
Student A: Thanks.

Student A: How much are the shorts?
Student B: They're $10.41.
Student A: Thanks.

F. **Study the chart.**

Singular	Plural
How much **is** the dress?	How much **are** the shoes?

G. Listen and write.

CD 1
TR 75-80

1. _$32.50_

2. _____

3. _____

4. _____

5. _____

6. _____

H. CONFIRM Ask a classmate for the prices in Exercise G. Write the receipts.

Adel's
Clothing Emporium

pants $32.50

Total $32.50
Customer Copy

Adel's
Clothing Emporium

shirt ..... _____
shoes .... _____

Total .... _____
Customer Copy

Adel's
Clothing Emporium

dress ..... _____
shorts .... _____
blouse .... _____

Total .... _____
Customer Copy

I. CREATE Speak to a partner. Ask for three items and complete the receipt.

Student A: How can I help you?

Student B: How much <u>are the pants</u>?

Student A: <u>$32.50</u>

Student B: Thanks. I want <u>two pairs</u>.

Student A: Great. Anything else?

Adel's
Clothing Emporium

_____ _____
_____ _____
_____ _____

Total .... _____
Customer Copy

LESSON 5 How much are the shoes?

GOAL ▉ Read advertisements

A. Read, listen, and write.

CD 1
TR 81

SAVE $5.00
ALL SIZES
$22.50

SAVE $12.00
SIZES 6-12

SALE
ALL SIZES
$33.00

SALE
ALL SIZES
$28.00

SAVE $4.00
ALL SIZES

SAVE $5.00
ALL SIZES

adel's
clothing emporium

B. Write.

1. How much are the shirts? $22.50

2. How much are the dresses?   _____

3. How much are the shoes?   _____

4. How much are the pants?   _____

C. RELATE Ask a classmate the questions in Exercise B.

D. Read.

How much and How many		
Question		**Answer**
How much	(money) is the sweater?	$33.00.
How much	is the shirt?	The shirt is $23.00.
How much	are the shoes?	They are / They're $40.00.
How many	coats do you want?	I want three coats.
How many	shirts do you want?	I want two shirts.

E. Practice the conversation. Use the information in Exercise A to make new conversations.

Student A: Can I help you?
Student B: Yes, I want <u>shirts</u>.
Student A: How many shirts do you want?
Student B: I want two shirts. How much are they?
Student A: They are <u>$22.50</u> each.

F. CLASSIFY Practice the conversation in Exercise E again. Speak to your classmates and take orders. (Use the ad in Exercise A.)

Name	Quantity (How many?)	Product	Price
Yusuf	two	shirts	$22.50

G. Read.

H. COMPARE Look at the ads for Norma's Fine Clothing and Adel's Clothing Emporium (Exercise A). Write the prices.

	Norma's Fine Clothing	Adel's Clothing Emporium
shirt	$24.00	$22.50
pants		
shoes		
dress		
sweater		

I. CREATE In a group, make an advertisement for a new clothing store. Practice the conversation from Exercise E.

LIFESKILLS ▶ That's a good deal

Before You Watch

A. **Look at the picture and answer the questions.**

1. Where are Hector and Mr. Sanchez?

2. What is Hector holding?

While You Watch

B. ▶ **Watch the video and fill in the missing prices.**

Item	Regular price	Sale price
jacket	$160	
coat		
pants		
tie		
shirt		

Check Your Understanding

C. **Put the sentences in order to make a conversation.**

a. _____ Clerk: What color?

b. _____ Customer: Yes, I need a new tie.

c. _____ Customer: That's nice. I'll take it.

d. _____1_____ Clerk: May I help you?

e. _____ Clerk: How about this one?

f. _____ Customer: Blue. It's for a job interview.

Review

Learner Log

I can identify types of clothing.
☐ Yes ☐ No ☐ Maybe

I can describe clothing.
☐ Yes ☐ No ☐ Maybe

A. Write the types of clothing.

1.
_____

2.
_____

3.
_____

4.
_____

5.
_____

6.
_____

7.
_____

8.
_____

B. Read and write.

1. We need three blue shirts. They are $18.59 each.

2. We need five green sweaters. They are $22.50 each.

3. We need one pair of black shoes. They are $33.00.

4. We need two red coats. They are $85.00 each.

Adel's Clothing Emporium			
Quantity (How many?)	Item	Color	Price
1.			$55.77
2.			$112.50
3.			$33.00
4.			$170.00

Learner Log

I can ask for and give directions in a store.   I can make purchases.

☐ Yes ☐ No ☐ Maybe   ☐ Yes ☐ No ☐ Maybe

C. Write the locations.

a. _It's in the corner of the store._

b. _____

c. _____

d. _____

e. _____

f. _____

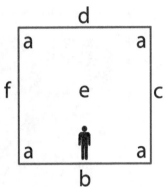

D. Which possible bills and coins do you need? Write.

Total	$20 bills	$10 bills	$5 bills	$1 bills	Quarters	Dimes	Nickels	Pennies
$69.00								
$22.50	1			2	2			
$56.90								
$132.00								
$153.75								
$113.80								

The Lincoln Memorial can be found on the back of the U.S. five-dollar bill.

E. Read the ad.

F. Write the information from the ad.

Item	Price	Savings
gray pants	$28.50	$5.00
jeans		
shirts		
blouses		
socks		
jackets		

TEAM PROJECT ✓ Open a clothing store

1. **COLLABORATE** Form a team with four or five students. In your team, you need:

Position	Job description	Student name
Student 1: Team Leader	Check that everyone speaks English. Check that everyone participates.	
Student 2: Writer	Make an inventory list.	
Student 3: Artist	Make an ad for a clothing store.	
Students 4/5: Spokespeople	Prepare a presentation.	

2. Make an ad.

3. Open a store. What is the name? Design the store.

4. Write an inventory list.

5. Present your store to the class.

The grand opening of a new store usually involves cutting a ribbon.

A Walk on the Wild Side

"You can't think, 'I still have 1,002 days to go, 995 days to go.' You'd get crazy. So, you live the moment."
—Sarah Marquis

A. PREDICT Look at the picture. Answer the questions.

1. Where is Sarah Marquis in the picture? What is she doing?

2. What clothes is she wearing? Why?

B. CLASSIFY Write the clothes people wear when it is hot and cold.

Hot	Cold

C. Read about Sarah Marquis.

Sarah Marquis is from Switzerland. She is an explorer who travels around the world *by foot*. In 2014, she was named as one of National Geographic's Adventurers of the Year for her walk from Siberia to Australia. She completed the journey in three years! After each adventure Sarah shares her stories. She walks in places like Siberia, Mongolia, and the Andes mountains in Peru. To explore cold countries like Canada, she has pants, sweaters, and coats. To explore warm countries like Australia, she has t-shirts. No matter where she goes, she always has her most important item of clothing—her shoes!

* by foot = to walk

D. IDENTIFY Underline the clothing in the story.

E. Scan the article and write the places Sarah has explored on the map.

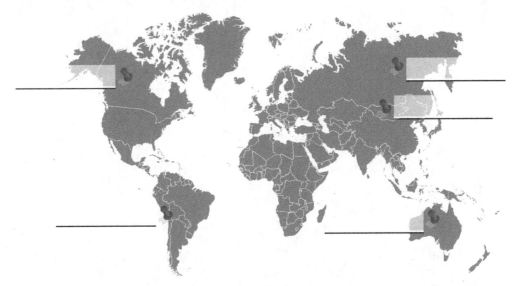

F. Read the article again. Answer the questions.

1. Where is it hot? _____

2. Where is it cold? _____

G. APPLY Complete the sentences about you and share with a partner.

1. I live in _____.

2. It is _____ (cold/warm/hot) most of the time.

3. I wear _____ a lot.

4. My favorite clothes are _____.